THE REAL STORY OF THE FLOOD

THE REAL STORY OF

THE FLOOD

by PAUL L. MAIER

Illustrated by Robert T. Barrett

CONCORDIA PUBLISHING HOUSE • SAINT LOUIS

Published by Concordia Publishing House
3558 S. Jefferson Avenue • St. Louis, MO 63118-3968
1-800-325-3040 • www.cph.org

Text © 2008 by Paul L. Maier
Illustrations © 2008 Concordia Publishing House

1 2 3 4 5 6 7 8 9 10   17 16 15 14 13 12 11 10 09 08

PROLOGUE

God created a perfect paradise. But man and woman fell into sin, and a general rot set in. Disease and death were not part of God's original plan, but now they infected the earth everywhere. Weeds cluttered the ground. Animals grew ferocious and fought among themselves. Human beings were the worst offenders: unlike the beasts, people disobeyed God and *knew* they were doing so, intentionally helping to ruin the divine creation as much as they possibly could with all their corruption and violence.

The Creator was angry! Perhaps He should simply give up on what He had created, destroy the world, and start all over again?

CHAPTER ONE

So the Lord said, "I will blot out man whom I have created from the face of the land, man and animals and creeping things and birds of the heavens, for I am sorry that I have made them."
Genesis 6:7

The Lord had many different ways to destroy life on earth. How about *fire*? A long string of mighty volcanic explosions from the earth's hot core could have smothered the world in flame. But what a horrible mess would be left!

How about *wind* and *storm*? Vast tornados and hurricanes across the globe could have toppled civilizations and swept away mankind. But, again, what a horrible mess would be left!

Perhaps *disease*—a worldwide epidemic of super viruses and bacteria to wipe out man and beast? or *famine* and *starvation*? The mess left behind by these catastrophes would be the worst of all!

God had a better solution: *water*. He had more than enough, since by His own design three-quarters of the earth's surface is water. And although floods can be messy, they would leave behind much less clutter than the other methods. Yes, the Creator would use water.

Still, there was one problem: was God disgusted with *everybody* on earth? Were there *any* exceptions?

CHAPTER TWO

But Noah found favor in the eyes of the Lord. . . . And God said to Noah, "Make yourself an ark." Genesis 6:8, 13

Indeed, there were! Amid the sea of wicked unbelievers was an island of faith in the family of a man named Noah. He was righteous in God's sight, and so was his wife, their three sons—Shem, Ham, and Japheth—and their wives. They were "the elite eight," whom the Creator had no reason to destroy. So He prepared a way for them to survive the mighty flood He was preparing.

"Noah, I want you to build an ark," said the Lord.

"Fine, Lord!…But…what's an ark?" Noah might have replied.

God not only explained the sort of ship He had in mind, but even gave Noah its dimensions. It was to be 450 feet long, 75 feet wide, and 45 feet high. It would have three decks, a roof, and a big door in its side.

A lesser man than Noah might have fainted at that news. The ark would be more than a hundred times the size of a ship needed to save only eight people. What in the world did God have in mind?

The Creator had no reason to be angry at beasts who could not reason, and so He would save the animal kingdom along with humanity itself through means of this ark. Noah was to prepare nothing less than a floating zoo to preserve life on earth.

CHAPTER THREE

"Make yourself an ark of gopher wood. Make rooms in the ark, and cover it inside and out with pitch." Genesis 6:14

They started to build the great ship according to divine design. Cypress was used for the ark's hull, since it was sturdy and often used in the ancient world for shipbuilding. To make the vessel watertight, Noah was to coat the hull inside and out with tarry pitch. There would be three decks— lower, middle, and upper—divided into rooms for people, stalls for animals, and storage for food of every variety necessary to feed the birds and animals aboard.

We can only imagine how Noah and his family must have been ridiculed by onlookers while building their ship. We can almost hear their taunts:

"Hey, fellas, what is that contraption anyway? It's too big for a boat, too small for a city…"

"Pathetic! Why don't you build that thing near water instead of this wheat field? If it's a ship, how're you ever going to *launch* it?"

"If you're going fishing, what do you hope to catch? Whales?"

And so on.

Maybe all the joking at their expense rattled Noah's sons as they sweated away at their huge task: felling trees, carving them into ribs or cutting them into boards, and finally hammering them into a hull. Might they even have doubted if their father had heard the Lord correctly?

CHAPTER FOUR

Noah did this; he did all that God commanded him. Then the Lord said to Noah, "Go into the ark, you and all your household, for I have seen that you are righteous before Me." Genesis 6:22–7:1

Noah himself had no doubts at all. Scripture tells us that he "was a righteous man, blameless among the people of his time, and he walked with God" (Genesis 6:9). Clearly, this was as close to the Creator as any creature could get. And if there were any family discussions about how the neighbors were making fun of the ark-building enterprise, Noah brushed it off and told Shem, Ham, and Japheth to get on with their work and ignore the ridicule.

We have no idea how long it took to build this huge ship, but construction went on and on. Slowly it took shape. With the hull intact, the sides reached to within 18 inches of the top, where a roof angled down across this gap to keep out the rain while permitting fresh, outside air and light to fill the ark, probably through windows. It was a good design. Would one expect anything less from God?

One wonderful day, the ark was finally finished, and Noah and his family loaded it with food and other provisions. But what about the animals who were supposed to come in pairs— male and female—to board the craft? It would have taken months to round up and capture all the species of animals, birds, and crawling creatures involved. Would this throw a wrench into God's plans?

CHAPTER FIVE

They went into the ark with Noah, two and two of all flesh in which there was
the breath of life. And those that entered, male and female of all flesh, went
in as God had commanded him. And the Lord shut him in. Genesis 7:15–16

"Build it, and they will come!" God must have told Noah.

And so it was. As the skies darkened ominously and the worst low-pressure system in the history of weather science formed over the earth, a magnificent menagerie appeared at Noah's ark. With incredible order, they lined up in pairs as they approached the big ramp that led to the middle deck of the ark: bellowing cattle, lumbering elephants, lofty giraffes, braying donkeys, barking dogs, and all their many relatives in the animal world.

How did they ever know to do this? How did they know where to go? Today we know that animals can sense an approaching catastrophe of some kind, such as an earthquake or tsunami, long before humans can with all their scientific instruments. And, of course, God Himself was in charge of this animal parade. It must have been a stunning sight for Noah and his brood, to say nothing of their nosy neighbors, whose taunts were not nearly as loud, now, as they had been.

When the last of the animals had boarded the ark and were led to their respective stalls, the great door was shut tight. Bystanders surely wondered what in the world was happening. Animals didn't act like that. The sky never looked like that. The air itself never felt like that. An eerie silence blanketed the earth that seemed worse than anything they had ever heard.

CHAPTER SIX

The waters increased and bore up the ark, and it rose high above the earth. Genesis 7:17

Worse was to come. The darkness suddenly flickered with blinding light as hundreds of lightning bolts seemed to strike the earth at the same time. Shattering explosions of thunder boomed everywhere. Torrents of rain poured down, quickly turning the field surrounding the ark into a soggy marsh.

"It's a terrible, terrible storm," onlookers must have thought. "But it'll blow over quickly."

Not this one. The rain, coming down in sheets, appeared to get worse, if that were possible. As the Bible puts it, "All the springs of the great deep burst forth, and the floodgates of the heavens were opened" (Genesis 7:11). No storm was ever like this one. Soon the fields were covered with a yard or two of water as Noah's ark suddenly launched itself. Drenched bystanders no longer stood at a distance and joked about the bulky, odd-looking ship; now they swam alongside it and desperately beat on its hull, trying to climb aboard. But God Himself had closed the door and it would not be opened.

Inside, Noah and his family could only thank the Lord for saving them from this watery catastrophe, and they broke out into hymns and prayers. Even their animal passengers, terrified by the horrendous storm, seemed glad to be high, dry, and—somehow—secure.

CHAPTER SEVEN

The flood continued forty days upon the earth. . . . The waters prevailed and increased greatly on the earth, and the ark floated on the face of the waters. Genesis 7:17–18

Day after day, week after week, the rain continued. This was no gullywasher, not even some regional flood. Creeks became rivers, while rivers long since swelled far beyond their banks. Lakes became seas, and finally the waters of the oceans poured in from the seashore to join them in furious foaming.

One morning, Noah and his crew looked out the window and saw no land at all— only a vast ocean of water surrounding their craft. The deluge covered the earth itself.

Because of the pelting, endless rain, Noah and his sons must have made a daily tour of the ark to check for leaks in the roof. Far more dangerous would be leaks in the hull, for they could sink the ship. But there were none: the tarry pitch was doing its job, and they had built their boat very well indeed. God's protection, of course, was an even more important reason.

For forty days and forty nights it went on—no sun, no moon, no stars—just endless clouds and the longest, most drenching rainstorm in history.

CHAPTER EIGHT

Only Noah was left, and those who were with him in the ark.
And the waters prevailed on the earth 150 days.
Genesis 7:23–24

All of this should have been depressing and terrifying for the crew aboard the ark. Since God had told Noah what would happen, however, he and his family were not frightened.

Instead, they were busy—*very* busy! All those animals had to be fed twice a day, and it had to be exactly the right food for each pair. Hay and grain would work well for many of the animals, but certainly not all. And birds would have to have a different menu entirely. The one group Noah and his family did not have to care for, of course, were fish and sea creatures, who may even have appreciated their expanded domain.

For those aboard the ark, water was no problem whatever during the forty-day deluge! But they collected it in great cisterns for the time when the rain would end, and it did end. Yet the water remained and the ark floated on—for the next *five months*!

CHAPTER NINE

*And Noah removed the covering of the ark and looked, and behold, the face
of the ground was dry. Genesis 8:13*

After you take a shower, the quickest way to dry your hair is to aim the hot blast of a hair-dryer on it. On an infinitely larger scale, God did the same thing after the flood. As the Bible tells us, "He sent a wind over the earth, and the waters…receded steadily" (Genesis 8:1, 3).

Soon the mountaintops broke onto the horizon, and the ark ran aground in the Ararat mountains, somewhere in what is today eastern Turkey. Should they open the ship's door and release their cargo of livestock, birds, and wild animals? Of course not! They would freeze at that altitude or drown in waters that still covered the valleys. So how was Noah to know the right time to exit the ark?

Very cleverly, he opened a window in the ship and released a dove to see if it could land anywhere. The dove returned, unable to find a spot to perch. A week later, Noah sent it out again. This time it returned with a fresh olive leaf in its beak. Since olive trees do not grow at high elevations, the bird virtually told Noah that water was receding even from the valleys. Just to be sure, Noah sent out the same bird a week later, but this time it did not return. The flood had ended; the earth had dried out.

When Noah looked out of the window of the ark, he could see for himself. There stood the mountains and the valleys with no water to be seen, except for the little lakes that had been there previously. It was a *beautiful* sight!

CHAPTER TEN

Then Noah built an altar to the LORD and . . . offered burnt offerings on the altar.
Genesis 8:20

Now they could safely leave their huge, wooden life-preserver so graciously specified by God. The ark had come to rest against a natural elevation on the mountainside that served as a perfect ramp for another parade, this time by beasts delighted to be free of their cramped stalls. Two by two, they scampered off in all directions to repopulate the world's animal kingdom. If they had been able, they would likely have thanked Noah for his maritime hospitality.

Noah and his family thanked God Himself, of course. First things first. Just after leaving the ark, Noah built a stone altar to the Lord and performed sacrifice in gratitude for His saving them all from a terrible, watery death.

For His part, God was pleased with Noah's righteous obedience and now made a colossal promise to him—and to all humanity: Never again would He destroy mankind through a flood or any other means. In beautiful poetry, the Lord put it this way:

> *As long as the earth endures,*
> *seedtime and harvest,*
> *cold and heat,*
> *summer and winter,*
> *day and night*
> *will never cease.*

And so it has been ever since.

CHAPTER ELEVEN

"Behold, I establish My covenant with you and your offspring after you, and with every living creature that is with you."
Genesis 9:9

God now made a "covenant" with Noah, all the humanity he represented, and even the animal world. A covenant is like a contract between people or agencies, but on a much higher level since this one was between the Creator and His creatures. God not only promised never again to destroy the living inhabitants of this planet, He even provided a guarantee for that promise: *the rainbow!*

Who but God Himself could have put it this way: "Whenever I bring clouds over the earth and the rainbow appears in the clouds, I will remember My covenant between Me and you and all living creatures of every kind. Never again will the waters become a flood to destroy all life" (Genesis 9:14).

How doubly beautiful, then, is the rainbow! It not only separates white light into its magnificent colors—red, orange, yellow, green, blue, indigo, and violet—but it guarantees God's promise to us all.

Finally, it was time for matters to get back to normal. In a world whose population had been destroyed, we can almost anticipate that God would give Noah and his family the same command He had given in the Garden of Eden: "Be fruitful and multiply, bring forth abundantly on the earth" (Genesis 9:7).

CHAPTER TWELVE

These three were the sons of Noah, and from these the people of the whole earth were dispersed. Genesis 9:19

The three sons of Noah—Shem, Ham, and Japheth—now had an awesome responsibility. They and their wives were to repopulate the earth. The aging Noah now turned to agriculture, planted vineyards, and invented wine-making.

The tenth chapter of the Book of Genesis gives us the "Table of the Nations," a cascade of names that descended from Noah. Astonishingly, the names of his three sons survive to this day as designations for some of the principal racial groups in the world!

Shem became the ancestor of the earth's "Shemites" or Semitic peoples, who would inhabit lands to the east of the Mediterranean Sea. Shem's great-grandson Eber became the father of the "Hebrews," named for him. In the very distant future, a descendant of Shem named Peter would compare Baptism with the flood (1 Peter 3:20–21). Just as the ark saved humanity through the waters, so Jesus would save humanity in the waters of Baptism through faith in His ministry, death, and resurrection.

The offspring of *Ham* would live in Egypt and North Africa, where the "Hamitic" peoples, again named for him, would prosper.

The descendants of *Japheth*, the youngest son, would settle in the north country: Asia Minor, and the coastlands of the Aegean, Black, and Caspian seas. "Japhethites" would eventually be called Aryan or Indo-European peoples, the ancestors of people who trace their roots to Europe.

The world would soon be repopulated indeed! The flood was now history.

EPILOGUE

"Wait a minute," you might be thinking. "This is certainly an interesting story, but *is* it history? Did it really happen? Did all of those animals really crowd onto one ship? Wouldn't dinosaurs crush Noah's ark if they tried to board it?"

The answer to these questions is…Yes. But Mr. and Mrs. Tyrannosaurus Rex missed the boat. They were not around at the time. Nor were their brontosaurus, triceratops, or stegosaurus relatives. All the gigantic citizens of Jurassic Park lived and died long *before* the flood. Indeed, they roamed the earth during that early era described in the first half of Genesis, chapter one.

It *is* history. In fact, many ancient civilizations have flood epics that parallel the biblical version. Among the Babylonians, the flood story was called the *Gilgamesh Epic*. In ancient Egypt, the annual flooding of the Nile River reminded people of a much greater deluge. In ancient Greece, it was not an ark but Mount Parnassus that enabled a couple at its summit to survive the Greek version of the flood. And in the Americas, the Mayans told their children of a great flood.

Will anyone ever find ruins of the ark? That remains to be seen, but whether the ark is ever found, you can be sure that the flood *did* happen! You have proof of it every time you see a rainbow.